Mastering Your Finance Volume 1

Paolo Debernardi

ISBN 978-1-915787-98-9

Printed in Great Britain by
Biddles Books Limited, King's Lynn, Norfolk

Contents

Introduction

I want to thank you for purchasing this book, *Mastering Your Finance Vol. 1*, the aim of which is to help you to better manage your finances by increasing your income and reducing your outgoings, resulting in better budgeting of your money. You might wonder why I should talk about managing better your finances? During my life, I have gained a diploma in Accountancy, worked as an Accountant Assistant and as a Finance Assistant, where my role involved budgeting the accounts every month. I have been immersed in Finance for most of my life - that is the reason I can help you to improve financially through my knowledge as an accountant and my experience. I have created a "seven steps" system from which, if my instructions are followed, people can achieve a better financial existence. I have put this system into practice in my financial life, and I have seen a radical transformation. I used to overspend every month but, after I implemented it, I have money in my bank account, reduced my debts and improved my credit score, without working more hours or having more than one job.

My name is Paolo Debernardi. I was born on 3 July 1973 at Casale Monferrato, Italy. I studied Accountancy in Italy for five years; despite my qualification, it is very difficult to find a job in Italy, so I moved to UK in 1997. Unfortunately, my Accountancy Diploma is not recognised in the UK, so I had no choice but to work as a cleaner, progressing to a shop assistant by upgrading my CV and gaining more skills and qualifications. I have learned that, if you develop yourself, you can move forward in your career. In fact, many years later, I started working in an office as Accountant Assistant. Most of my jobs were temporary; I have had more than 65 of them in 25 years and, even when I have been offered a permanent job, the company was dissolved, resulting in me being made redundant. On other occasions, I was discriminated against due to my nationality, but it did not discourage me and I kept going. I even went through a divorce which lasted three and a half years (I was only married for one year), losing my flat and my job. I was homeless, jobless and penniless, with debts. My positive mindset helped me to get through. Within a week, I found accommodation and a job and, years later, my financial position was improving. Covid 19 came, and it made me realise that this was an opportunity for me to reset my life, cutting down my expenses, budgeting my finances better, reducing my debts and reevaluating the way I relate to money.

In fact, lots of people do not have a good relationship with money; as soon as they start earning, through a salary or a business, they have already found ways to get rid of the hard-earned cash. Every decision you make, every day, has an impact on your life and a positive or negative change in the value of your finances, in direct relation to how you use your money. Previously, I spent money without thinking about the future consequences; however, since Covid 19 has impacted my life, I think about money as an asset. Rich people are rich because they make their money work for them, and they manage their money better. A proportion of the money I received I started to invest and save, with the aim of earning a passive income (a passive income is generated by an asset, like an investment or property, where you do not need to work to receive a payment). The rest is used to pay my personal expenses (bills, groceries, and public transport).

One myth is that getting a better salary through a job, or income through a business, will mean that you have more money to cover your personal expenses. However, you are going to spend more money as your disposable income grows, and you try to match your income with your personal expenses. It is your subconscious which is dictating how you should live your life. I used to behave the same way as everyone else, but I changed my mindset and my finance has improved by reducing my outgoings and managing my money better. The transformation needs to be within yourself; it does not matter how many books you read, or what courses you study. The only way to move forward is changing the way you think, implementing what you learn, taking actions every day which will result in changes in your life. You might not see immediate results - the compound effect takes time to show results.

An example: I wanted to lose weight; I did not like my appearance when I was staring at the bathroom mirror, so I decided to take action. Every day I was eating healthy food for breakfast and walking for 20 miles delivering newspapers, which helped me to earn money, keep fit and lose weight, all at the same time. For the first 3 months I did not see any external changes but, internally my body had already changed and, three months later, I had lost so much weight I needed to buy a new, shorter belt because my trousers did not fit me anymore.

As you can see, changing your mindset plus taking daily actions = results.

I am very confident that, if you follow my seven steps system with the correct mindset, you too will transform your finances, as long as you keep doing it every single day. If you are ready to start your new journey, turn the page to Step 1. Congratulations for taking this journey.

Step 1

Congratulations again for taking this journey.

> "No matter where you are right now, you can change your financial position; as long as you have a positive mindset, set up goals and take daily actions, your life will transform, and your finances will improve."
>
> *Paolo Debernardi.*

Before we start, we need to change our mindset, otherwise we learn new skills, new ways, but we have not improved our lives, because we have not transformed, or we make the New Year resolutions which are lasting for only a short period of time. My aim is to help you to be a better version of you, so the impact of the changes has a radical transformation.

"What is a mindset? Your Mindset is a set of beliefs that shape how you make sense of the world and yourself. It influences how you think, feel, and behave in any given situation. It means that what you believe about yourself impacts your success or failure." If you search on Google, this definition will come up. Your Mindset is referring not only to a business; it can be also related to losing weight, budgeting your finances better, or improving your personal relationships with other people. Your Mindset can be used for any situation. You need to have a strong Mindset and, when you have, you can overcome any difficult situations.

Many years ago, I started working in a company as a Purchase Ledger clerk in the first month of the new job. The company had hired a new manager, who was not very supportive of new employees and kept some approved invoices to be paid. Despite my experience and knowledge, every day I struggled to work in this Finance Department, due to my awkward manager who was making my working life difficult, so I was not surprised when I did not pass my probation. I was devasted but, thanks to my strong Mindset, I was determined to find a new job, otherwise I would not be able to pay my personal expenses because I was running out of money. I put a plan into action: I emailed my CV to all the recruiting agencies and applied for 20 jobs every day until I was offered a new job. Within a week, I started a new job. This shows the formula works: Mindset plus daily activities = results.

If I break it down to my personal experience: Mindset + sending emails to all the recruiting agencies + applying for jobs = a new job being offered to me (result).

How can you strengthen your Mindset? Every day you are facing problems in your life and negative thoughts appear in your mind. You need to replace one negative thought with 3 positive ones. In my example, I had just lost my job, and I was upset and worried. I knew I had lot of experience and that I could find a job very easily. Even if I overcame this situation the manager had created, the manager would find a different excuse to get rid of me. In the end, I was pleased I learned from this experience, and I am now better version of me. I replaced my negative thoughts (anger, upset) with positive thoughts (a good employee, a problem solver, an accountant). Positive thoughts create a positive attitude, which attracts positive results.

You also need to be surrounded by positive people. We cannot avoid negative people, like our family, or some of our friends and acquaintances, but we can spend less time with them. Positive people bring knowledge, experience and a brighter vision, with infinite possibilities. Positive people also usually have a higher income, which can help you to develop and grow mentally and financially.

Your Mindset can be affected by positive affirmation, which can help you every day. For example, if you say, "I am good at playing sports," and "I am not good at budgeting my finances." Both affirmations are correct, because you are telling your subconscious you believe what you are. You can change your subconscious even though, right now, you are not good at managing your finances by just saying you are good at managing your finances. You are learning and improving every day. Over time you will be budgeting your finances better. This is very important to change all your affirmations to positive, and your Mindset will be stronger and more positive. Even when you are facing problems, you will overcome them with ease. Repeat your positive affirmation after you wake up and before you go to sleep.

For example: "I am a money magnet; I am a positive person; I can do this."

You are an amazing person; do not allow others to bring you down. Believe in yourself even more when things are not going your way.

Another way you can improve your Mindset is by reading self-improvement books, like *Think and Grow Rich*, by Napoleon Hill, *The Power of Your Subconscious Mind*, by Dr Joseph Murphy, and *You Were Born Rich*, by Bob Proctor.

Reading these books will help you to grow and think in a positive way. You also need to change your current habits or beliefs to make an impact in your life. If you practise a new habit consciously every day for 21 days in a row, you can change your attitude. Some habits will take longer than 21 days to become part of your life. The secret is carrying on until the new habit becomes part of you. The following book explains why we do what we do and how to change: *The Power of Habit* by Charles Duhigg.

I totally agreed with this affirmation:

> "The person you will be in five years is based on the books you read and the people you surround yourself with today."

Simon Stepsys

To implement what you have learned so far, please follow this simple exercise:

1) Read, for 15 minutes in the morning after you wake up and 15 minutes before you go to sleep, the books that have been mentioned in this chapter.

2) If you have a negative thought, replace it immediately with 3 positive affirmations (e.g., "I believe in myself," "I can achieve anything in life," and "I am good at managing my money.")

3) Be surrounded by, and talk and listen to, positive people.

When you have mastered Step 1, you are ready for Step 2.

Step 2

Congratulations on mastering Step 1, you are doing a good job; keep going. Without Mindset, you will not succeed in budgeting your finances better. This step I am talking about is setting goals. So, what is a goal-setting? The **definition** of **goal-setting** is the process of identifying something that you want to accomplish and establishing measurable **goals** and timeframes. When you decide on a financial change to save more money, and then set a certain amount to save each month, this is an example of **goal-setting**.

1) Justify your 'why' as your driving factor to achieve your goal. If your 'why' is not strong enough, i.e., lack of a positive Mindset, your actions will not support you to reach your goal. You need to have a clear idea of what you want to achieve. The starting point of all achievement is desire. Keep this constantly in mind. Weak desire brings weak results:

   "Just a small fire makes a small amount of heat."
   Napoleon Hill

2) Each day, write down a plan of action you have to follow to achieve your goal. If you plan each day, you will succeed in achieving your goals, e.g., saving money monthly. If you do not plan, you are going to fail.

3) Bring your 'why' back when you are facing tough times.

4) Read the books listed below, for supporting you and giving you strength during your attempts to achieve your goals:
   Think and Grow Rich, by Napoleon Hill
   The Power of Your Subconscious Mind, by Joseph Murphy
   You Were Born Rich, by Bob Proctor
   How to Win Friends and Influence People, by Dale Carnegie

The 90 Day Challenge, by Simon Stepsys

Your goals need to be smart: specific, measurable, attainable, realistic and timely.

> "When it is obvious that the goals cannot be reached, don't adjust the goals, adjust the action steps."
>
> *Confucius.*

> "When you're breaking a goal down into individual tasks and activities, you'll easily lose focus or get distracted. All the little things you need to do to get there will discourage you and you might want to give up. This is where you can use your 'why' as a tool to keep yourself motivated and on track."
>
> *Simon Stepsys*

> "The person you will be in five years is based on the books you read and the people you surround yourself with today."
>
> *Simon Stepsys.*

In the last step I talked about losing the purchase ledger role.

My mindset was positive, so I knew I would find a job. I have a strong desire to work and earn (that is my 'why' as my driving factor) because, if I am not earning, I cannot pay the bills.

I wrote a plan each day to achieve my goal in finding a new role. In my diary, I wrote tasks and activities to break down my goal. I got up at 8 am each day, phoned all the agencies in York and Leeds and emailed my CV. If the action I took did not bring any results, I applied for 50 jobs each day online until I had been invited to interviews and, ultimately, a new employer would offer me a position.

My tasks and activities had paid off, as I had been offered a new role.

To recap

Follow this exercise:

1) Justify your 'why' as your driving factor to achieve your goal.

2) Each day, write down a plan of action which you have to follow to achieve your goal.

3) Break down a goal into individual tasks and activities.

4) Bring your 'why' back when you are facing tough times.

5) Read the books which have been listed for supporting you and giving you strength during your attempts to achieve your goals.

Step 3

Congratulations on mastering Step 2, you are doing a good job; keep going. In this chapter, I am going to talk about budget. So, what is a budget?

The **definition** of **budget** is "an estimate of income and expenditure for a set period of time."

Budget is very important for individuals and companies because, if you are not budgeting your finances, you will be struggling to pay your bills and pay for your food, causing stress and worries for you and your family.

Every month you receive your latest bank statement, which shows all the money coming in and going out of your bank account.

Write down on a piece of paper, or type in an Excel spreadsheet, on the left side, all the money coming in: your salary, your partner's salary, any benefits you receive, profits coming from a business, etc.

On the same piece of paper or Excel document, on the right side, write or type all the money coming out from your bank account: ATM withdrawals, gas and electricity bills, insurance premiums, mobile phone charges, landline and internet, Council Tax, rent or mortgage, public transport, petrol or diesel for a car, car insurance, TV licence, house insurance, credit cards and loan repayments, groceries and so on. These are the most common liabilities for individuals. It is also a good idea to include the company you are paying, because later you can compare with other companies which are offering the same service or products. If another company charges less, you can switch, save money and improve your finances.

After you have completed this exercise, add all the left-side positive values and the right-side negative values. When you have all the totals, the income total should be higher than the outgoings total. You have money left over after paying the bills.

If your totals are the same, something needs to be changed because, if the cost of living increases, you will not have any money to pay your bills. In this case, you need to re-evaluate how to reduce all your expenditures so as to avoid not having enough money in your bank account.

If your outgoing total is higher than your income total, you need to make changes in your life to master your finances.

One myth is stopping payment of subscriptions like *Sky* or *Amazon*. Temporarily, you would reduce your outgoings because you would have more money in your bank account. However, we tend to spend the extra cash we have. If you want to budget your finances better, you need to tackle your entire financial situation.

In the case of the *Sky* subscription, I am currently using this company and I called them because I was aware that, in future months, my fixed contract would expire, resulting in an increased bill. They offered me a new fixed contract for a certain amount of time, to keep the cost down and allowing me to budget my finances. If you still require their services, my best tip is: **contact all the companies you pay every month and set up an amount you are comfortable with paying**.

Other people spend money on take-aways. Apart from the fact that take-away food is not good for you, it is also very expensive. In my life, I prefer to spend this money in a supermarket. You can buy more food and I know what I am eating. If you stop spending money on take-aways, this action alone will reduce your outgoings. Talking about supermarkets, I used to shop in the Co-op, which was more expensive than Lidl. Lidl has helped me to budget my finances better. In other circumstances, shopping with different supermarkets can help you to reduce your utility bills, which I cover in Step 4.

When you travel to go to work, you can travel either by car or on public transport. My preference is for public transport, because it helps me to budget. Other people prefer a car; driving a car, however, is very expensive way to travel. Apart from the purchase of the vehicle, usually in instalments, you need to add the cost of car insurance, fuel, parking, and repair or maintenance of the car. Every day, we are bombarded by TV or Internet commercials; we are also influenced by other external factors, like if we have had a bad day, so we are looking for comfort food or clothes to cheer us up. But we should ask ourselves whether we really need to buy it. If the answer is no, walk out of the shop.

Before, I used to spend money without thinking and, later, finding myself struggling to pay my utility bills.

Now I am aware of all my direct debits, and other bills which need to be paid. Before I make any purchases, I check whether I have enough money in my bank account to cover all my bills, and if I can afford to make the purchase. If I can't, I walk away.

Before I moved to my own place, I was renting a room which was not big enough for all furniture and belongings, so I had no choice but to put all my belonging into storage, paying £78 a month for 7 years. I was very shocked that I had paid over £6000 in storage fees and, as soon as I could, I took out all my belongings from the storage to my own place, saving me £78 monthly. **Another good tip is always to check your bank statements, making sure you are not paying a company which is no longer selling you a service or product.**

With regard to the utility bills, I will cover them in Step 4, and I will talk about credit cards and loans in Step 5.

To recap

Follow this monthly exercise:

1) Each month, write down on a piece of paper, or type in an Excel document, all the money coming in to, and going out of, your bank account, including ATM withdrawals. Compare the totals in each column.

2) If the total outgoings are equal to, or higher than, your total income, reduce your outgoings.

3) Keep budgeting every day as you become better, and you will be in control of your finances.

In the next step, I will talk about how to reduce your utility bills.

Step 4

Congratulations on mastering Step 3, you are doing a good job; keep going. In this chapter, I am going to talk about reducing your utility bills. Before you decide to change your energy providers, there are other ways to reduce your electricity and gas consumption.

My first tip is installing solar panels and storage batteries, if you are the homeowner. Since I have installed solar panels in my property, my electricity consumption has been reduced every month and, during the summer season, I have noticed that I have exported more electricity to the grid, resulting in a reduction in my electricity costs. My solar panels have the latest technology so that, even when it is overcast, my solar panels are still exporting electricity. I have been advised to use my washing machine during the day; that way, I am not consuming electricity because of my solar panels. During night-time, I am consuming electricity stored in the batteries.

Do not forget to send your electricity provider your exported electricity meter readings in kilowatt-hours every month.

My second tip is putting a net around the solar panels, otherwise the pigeons will create a nest if there is enough gap between your roof and the solar panels. I have this issue and I am glad I resolved it. **The third tip is to instal deterrent devices on your roof if pigeons are pooing in your gutters.** My solution was contacting a company which installed these devices; these scared the pigeons away and resolved another issue of pigeons sitting on my TV aerial and disrupting the TV signal. If you are interested in learning more about solar panels, please do not hesitate to contact me; you will save money, help the environment and earn up to £7500 for referring people to use the same company that installed my solar panels.

I am not sure if you are aware, but we are losing so much heat from our properties through the windows and external doors, so are using the central heating more during the winter, because the windows and doors have not been upgraded. The latest windows and doors are filled with argon, which helps to retain 70% of your heating in the property. If you are a homeowner, you would reduce your central heating costs and increase the value of your property.

Also, by 2028 you would have to adhere to legislation by the UK Government if you own a buy-to-let property. All the windows must be to energy rating C, otherwise the buy-to-let property cannot be rented out.

Currently, some people are heating their properties during winter using electric heaters; however, I have a better solution which would help everyone to reduce their consumption of electricity and gas.

Electric heaters vs oil heaters

If you live in a property which does not have central heating, or you are using an electric heater in the bathroom, you are currently using more electricity than you should. The electric heaters are warming the cold air in the room and, when the cold air warms up, it becomes lighter and moves to the ceiling. Then the warm air becomes cold again and the cycle restarts, and this is the reason why electric heaters consume more electricity, and it costs more to heat your property. Many years ago, I discovered oil heaters, which work much better than electric heaters. Oil heaters warm up all the air in a room within five minutes, consuming less electricity and resulting in a reduction of electricity costs. Oil heaters, being on wheels, can be moved to other rooms, and they can help to reduce the consumption of central heating.

I am glad I have installed smart meters, for both electricity and gas. Previously, my bills were always estimated, but now I know how much I am consuming, which helps me to be in control of my finances.

Since 2011, I have been with this company, because it is the only company in the UK that can help you to reduce your utility bills. If you would like to know more, please contact me. In the meantime, I will explain the reasons why I have chosen this company:

1) It notifies me, three weeks in advance, how much my utility bill is going to be, helping me to budget my finances better.

2) It provides many services: electricity, gas, landline and Internet, mobile phone, insurance. The more services I use, the more I save. I have taken 5 services and I am a gold customer. I will receive free lightbulbs as long as I remain a customer. This offer has already expired; however, the company brings out new offers every year.

3) As a customer, I save more money on my utility bills by using a charge card. Every time I shop at Sainsbury's or Asda, 3% cashback on my shopping will reduce my utility bills. I can use this charge card for shopping online or offline. The percentage of the cashback on purchases depends on the partner retailer. Each cashback will reduce my utility bills.

4) It provides many services. If you bank with Santander and open a 123 Bank account or a 123 lite bank account, and you become a customer of this company and pay your utility bill by direct debit, Santander will credit your account with 3% cashback from your utility bill. You need to set up another direct debit with another provider and credit your account with a salary every month. There is a charge for this service, although the cashback has always been higher than the charge. If you do not become a customer of this company, Santander will give you only 2% cashback.

5) When you become a customer of this company, you have an option to become a partner, which allows you to earn a passive

income, qualify for free holidays and receive a free mini-car, depending on your efforts and team efforts.

6) This company is a British company, and it has been operating for more than 40 years.

7) It is the company in the UK whose aim is to help consumers to save money on their bills.

To recap

follow this exercise:

1) If you are a homeowner, instal solar panels and upgrade your windows and external doors with the latest technology.

2) Replace electric heaters with oil heaters if you notice that consumption of your electric and gas is more than you can afford.

3) Contact with to become a customer with this utility company whose aim is to help you to reduce your utility bills and make money at the same time.

In the next step, I will talk about credit cards and loans.

Step 5

Congratulations on mastering Step 4, you are doing a good job; keep going. Before we talk about credit cards and loans, you need to understand the definition of Compound Effect.

So, what is Compound Effect? The **definition** of **Compound Effect** is reaping huge rewards from a series of small, smart choices. Success is earned in the moment-to-moment decisions that, in themselves, make no visible difference whatsoever; but the accumulated compounding effect is profound.

An example of compound effect is depositing money in your bank account. Each day your investment will generate interest which is going to be paid monthly or yearly. This is a **positive Compound Effect,** as it creates a reward.

Another example of compound effect is spending money on your credit card. Each time you make a purchase, it creates an outstanding balance you owe to the credit card company, which calculates interest on your purchases. Both balance and interest need to be paid back to the credit card company. In this case, the **Compound Effect** is **negative,** as it is a liability.

However, not all purchases are bad. Some of them are good debts, and others are bad debts.

Credit cards, loans and mortgages are also called "Other People's Money." So, what is Other People's Money?

The **definition** of **Other People's Money** is money you borrow from banks, credit card companies, credit unions, or investors. You must pay back the capital plus the interest at a certain date to clear the balance.

We need to distinguish **Bad Debt** from **Good Debt**. **Bad Debt** is purchasing holidays, groceries, clothes, etc. **Good Debt** is buying assets like **properties** or **businesses**, which increase in value over time and produce an income during the time you own the asset.

If you currently owe money to banks, credit unions, or other institutions, the first step is to identify what is the value of the outstanding debt, then the interest rate of the loan or credit card, and then the monthly repayment.

After you have identified all your liabilities and written them down, make sure that you pay the minimum payment to each one every month. It will reduce the amount of money you owe and it will increase your credit score. This is vital, as you will be able to borrow money in the future.

You will be able to obtain a mortgage and purchase a buy-to-let property.

I am not a financial adviser; I am giving you my suggestions. You need to check your circumstances. I am going to share my experience so that you can avoid the mistakes I have made in the past.

Please do not make my mistake; in the past, I needed a quick loan to buy an asset, but the interest rate was very bad, at 78% APR. However, I checked my budget to see if I could afford it. I was able to make the repayments. In addition, my monthly repayments helped me to improve my credit score and obtain another loan a year later at 15% APR, which cleared off the higher interest rate loan and thus saving me money and time.

You can register for free to check your credit score at: www.clearscore.com

Another strategy is to obtain a credit card at 0% APR, Barclaycard for example, and then transfer the balance you owe from another credit card, Capital One for example, at 38%, to Barclaycard at 0% and making the same repayments to Barclaycard instead of Capital One, £100 for example. Please check when the 0% offer ends and aim to clear off the balance before the normal interest rate starts from Barclaycard.

You will be able to clear off the balance of Barclaycard faster as you are paying £100 monthly with 0% APR, and you have cleared off the balance of Capital One because of the transfer.

Keep all the credit cards which have the best interest rate, 0% APR for example, because you can use them in the future for purchasing assets.

They are free cash available to you. If you clear the balance and then do not use them, eventually the credit card company will close your account.

If you currently own a property, you can borrow money against the property and pay off the loans and credit cards, as the mortgage is at a very low interest rate, saving you money and time in the long run.

Be careful, though, if borrowing money on a property - it is also risky. If you cannot pay back the mortgage, your property is at risk of being repossessed. However, you can sell the property and pay off the mortgage.

I would recommend these books:

about credit cards - *Guide to Becoming Rich*, by Robert Kiyosaki;

and about property - *Solving the Property Puzzle*, by Gill Fielding.

My Case Study

As you are aware, I had been through a divorce, that left me with lots of debts which were difficult to pay back until I implemented my 7-step system. Within the last 3 years I have cleared 8 debts, one of which was charging me £190.42 a month with 50% APR. I cleared this debt 3 months before the end of the contract. I was able to achieve this result because I cancelled one of the direct debits, which was a £78-a-month storage charge, with the result that I had more money going into my bank account.

The consequence of this action was that I was able to utilise the saving against another debt. It is like a chain reaction. Imagine a ball of string of debts; when you pay off one debt, your efforts can be redirected to the next debt, until it has been cleared. Most of the credit card companies or financial institutions expect that you would be making repayments on each of the debts in proportion to its size. However, each debt has a different monthly charge and APR. The best strategy is to pay off the highest monthly repayment and APR first, so that you can use the money you save for the next debt, which has the second highest monthly repayment and APR. If you follow the instructions from the financial institutions, it will take you longer to clear all your debts.

The other problem is that my income is below the British national average salary, so I cannot stretch my money to pay off all my debts. Another solution is contacting a debt management company; however, I had a bad experience. One company promised me that it would contact all my creditors and pay my debts. The reality is that they did not and, therefore, I started to deal with all the debts personally, so I know my debts are paid every month.

The other solution is applying for an Individual Voluntary Arrangement (IVA), where you agree with your creditors a payment which is more affordable and, after 5 years, all your debts have been written off. Your credit score will be affected, and you might lose your job if you are working in the financial sector; furthermore, if you cannot make your agreed repayments, you might be declared bankrupt. In my case, I have made so much effort on repaying my debts and improving my credit score, and jobs are not easily available for me, so I am not taking risks for my future.

There is another reason why my action would be better for you - your credit score will improve and you could obtain a better loan, or credit card, which has a lower APR. You can use this new debt, with its lower interest rate, to pay off the highest interest rate. This is also a strategy called "double header". You keep paying the minimum amount towards your debts every month until you notice that, after you have paid all your monthly outgoings, you have some spare cash. The common mistake is to carry on paying off your debts with the spare cash. The best way is to start investing in a cash ISA until you reach a sum of £5,000. The next step is to invest £5,000 into a British company which modernises properties (*Mastering Your Finance* Vol. 4) and return your capital with 11% profit each year. The final step is to keep growing your money until you have enough to purchase a buy-to-let property, resulting in an increase in value of the property over time, and rent from tenants monthly. This is the best strategy, because you will be able to clear your debts and have money in the future to top up your pension. If you do not follow this strategy and you just pay your debts every month and every year, it will take you such a long time and, when you retire, you will have only the State Pension and, possibly, a private pension to live on.

To recap

Follow this exercise:

1) Identify, in your bank account or saving account, the **positive Compound Effect**, which is the interest earned monthly or yearly.

2) Identify, in your credit card, loan or mortgage, the **negative Compound Effect**, which is the interest charged monthly.

3) Distinguish **bad debt** and **good debt** on your credit cards statement.

4) List all your credit cards, loans and/or mortgages with amounts outstanding, repayments and interest rates APR.

5) Make the minimum payment for each loan, credit card and mortgage. If you can afford more than a minimum, that is great. Do not miss a payment, otherwise the company charges you a £12 fee, and it affects your credit score for future borrowings.

6) Tackle the higher interest rate borrowings using credit card(s) at 0%, and transfer the balance or lower the interest rate, for example 78%, from the previous lender to 15% APR with a different lender.

7) Read Robert Kiyosaki's and Gill Fielding's books.

In the next step, I will talk about how to increase your income.

Step 6

Congratulations on mastering step 5, you are doing a good job; keep going. In this chapter, I talk about how to increase your income.

Robert T Kiyosaki has created cashflow quadrants, the first of which is called **Employee**.

So how do you increase your income?

Income is money received, especially on a regular basis, for work by your employer or through investment. You can increase your income by working more hours and/or overtime, especially at weekends or after your normal working hours. Your salary can increase when you are promoted in the company you are working for, or by receiving a company bonus.

You can also increase your income if you have a second job during your spare time, or if you leave your current role and work for another employer for a better salary.

Unfortunately, you are trading your time for money, and most workers will never be rich having a job, because their income is below the national average (£26000).

Pros: you have guaranteed income, pension and benefits.

Cons: the company can make you redundant, your employer can fire you, you need to ask permission for holidays, you are just a number to the company and all your efforts will benefit the company and its CEO, rather than yourself.

You can gain more qualifications and experience, which can open doors to better roles and better salaries.

In my life, I have experienced changes and improvements. Back in 1997, when I moved to the UK from Italy, I was an Italian accountant; however, my qualification is not recognised in the UK. My first job was as a cleaner. A friend of mine recommended that I should improve my CV.

The change resulted in gaining experience in working in shops and an office in 1998. For the last 25 years, I have been working in international companies. In the beginning, most of my roles were temporary contracts and, even when I had been offered permanent contracts, most of the companies had cashflow problems which resulted in redundancies.

I have learned not to be dependent on one source of income, because even permanent jobs are no more secure nowadays, and it is wise to be learning new skills and to be adaptable to any working environment, so that you can be effective as soon as you start your new role.

I have learned that, no matter where you are in life, you can make changes. If you are not making any changes, you are not in control. A long time ago, my grandmother was receiving her pension, and spent some of it on groceries. However, when Italy joined the European Union, the cost of living doubled and she was able to buy only half as much food as before, because the price of food doubled and her pension did not increase.

Do not rely on your current income to help you to survive in the future, because the cost of living can go up and you cannot do anything to increase your pension if you have not put in place other investments to top up your pension for the future.

To recap, follow this exercise:

1) Gain more skills and experience.

2) Work overtime or get promoted.

3) Look for a better salary in another company.

4) Have a second income.

Now I am moving to the next cashflow quadrant, which is called **Self-employment**. Another way to increase your income is to start a new business which is a person's regular occupation, profession, or trade. The first objective is to make sure that you are in profit from your business. This profit will pay you a wage. The profit is calculated from the revenue, minus costs of the business and tax to the government.

Pros: the advantage of the business is that you have total control of the business. You can take time off and you can build your business up. There is no limit to your income, unlike what you usually find in a regular job, and you do not need to ask permission from your employer for holidays. Another advantage is that you can claim travel expenses and subsistence, reducing your costs of the business. The travel expenses and subsistence cannot be claimed when you have a job.

Cons: there is no guarantee of income, like in a job and, when you are running a business, your business incurs some expenses. You need to manage your business cashflow, making sure your business is in profit so you can draw an income.

It seems daunting to start a new business; if you Google online, there are so many businesses advertised. Beware, though; some of them are sale pages and some of the others need to be avoided, but there are also good ones. In addition, you do not know if the business owner can run a business properly. So how do you know? Since 2014, I have been testing all the businesses online.

I have grouped all the best 20 businesses which pay me every month in a platform, so you have peace of mind; you earn money. It costs only £30 to get access. Anyone can follow my training and be successful. The risk is low, and the return is high.

Of course, you can Google and take a risk in joining a different business. My best advice is to make sure that, when you invest any money, you withdraw the same amount of money, so you are breaking even whatever happens to the business.

So, what are the costs of running a business? To run a business, you need only a laptop and the internet. My advice is not to lease premises or a shop until your business can generate enough cashflow to afford it.

Business online is the way forward, because you do not need to hire people, stock products, or have a physical location; all these three entities will reduce your profits. Do not get discouraged; you can make money online, just learn from successful people who are making money every day and making sure the successful entrepreneur can help you with training and knowledge so you can copy his or her activities and be successful too.

To recap, follow this exercise:

1) Join an established business online, knowing the business owner.

2) Gain training and knowledge so you become successful.

3) Claim your travel and subsistence expenses, thereby reducing the costs of the business.

4) Make sure you make a profit - revenue minus the costs of running of the business.

The next cashflow quadrant is called **Business owner**. Another way to increase your income is by starting a new business which is a person's regular occupation, profession, or trade. The first objective is to make sure that you are in profit from your business. This profit will pay you a wage. The profit is calculated from the revenue, minus costs of the business and tax to the government.

Pro: the advantage of the business is that you have total control of the business. You can take time off and you can build your business up. There is no limit to your income, which you usually find in a regular job, and you do not need to ask permission from your employer for holidays. Another advantage is that you can claim travel expenses and subsistence, reducing the costs of the business. The travel expenses and subsistence cannot be claimed when you have a job. This business will be successful because, as a business owner, you are leveraging all the employees' efforts to make the best and profitable business, if the employees are working efficiently and they are not wasting resources.

Cons: there is no guarantee of income like in a job and, when you are running a business, your business incurs some expenses. You need to manage your business cashflow, making sure your business is in profit, so you can draw an income. This business requires an investment of capital, as you need to lease premises, pay staff, pay suppliers, and buy or lease IT equipment, before you take this big step. I strongly recommend reading the book *Tycoon*, by Peter Jones.

The book covers every aspect of the business, so you are starting in the right way. I read it and it was so inspirational and helpful. The next step is to apply all the information from the book.

When you have created a business plan, you can approach banks or investors, or save money every month, to start a new business.

To recap, follow this exercise:

1) Read *Tycoon*, by Peter Jones.

2) Apply all the information of the book.

3) Create a business plan.

4) Borrow other people's money, or save money each month for your business.

Now I am moving to the last cashflow quadrant, which is called Investor. Income is money received, especially on a regular basis through investment. Another way to increase your income is to buy assets. So, what is an asset? It is an item of property owned by a person or a company, regarded as having value and available to meet debts, commitments, or legacies.

The best assets are **properties, gold** and **silver.** Gold and silver are very rare and are not in abundance. The value is always rising, and people tend to buy them more during a recession.

Properties are also very good assets, because the value of the property increases over time, and it can also generate a passive income through rent.

In 20 years' time in the UK there will be more renters than owners, due to the increase in the price of property and the slow increases in salary.

Before buying an asset, you need to gain knowledge and experience by the company which will teach individuals how to be successful and avoid all mistakes.

The next step is to raise the finance for purchasing the asset. You can use credit cards for the deposit (good debt), and a mortgage for the property.

If your credit is not very good, you need to first improve your credit score and save money every month. If you buy a property to live in, and pay your mortgage for 25 years until it is repaid, the deeds are placed with a bank or financial institution. The bank or financial institution cannot repossess your property if you make your mortgage repayments every month. However, if a person fails to make the mortgage repayments, then the bank has no choice but to repossess the property - if it did not take this action, there would be a financial crisis which would affect everyone.

You can build a portfolio of buy-to-let properties and use the refinance on the other properties to purchase your property mortgage for free.

To recap, follow this exercise:

1) Select your asset: gold, silver or property.

2) Gain more knowledge and experience by the asset company.

3) Borrow other people's money, or save money each month for the purchase of your asset.

Step 7

Congratulations on mastering step 6, you are doing a good job; you have completed all the steps. Keep doing all the steps every day and month, and you will achieve your goal of mastering your finances. You will reduce your debts and you will have money left in your bank account. When you have achieved this result, open a cash ISA with your bank. You will earn interest every day, and this cash ISA is an account for emergency use only. Instead of using a credit card, which charges high interest, you can use a cash ISA and transfer the amount of money you need into your bank account. Later, you can add the money you transferred into the cash ISA, and keep depositing until you reach £5,000. When you reach £5,000, please follow my instructions in *Mastering Your Finance* Vol. 4.

If you have any questions about my 7-step system, do not hesitate to contact me. I invite people to my five-day finance challenge on Zoom, where I answer all the questions and go more deeply into each step. I also provide one-to-one Zoom reviews on your finances, so I can help you to tackle your finances efficiently and formulate a strategy which will be tailored to solve any financial problems you are facing currently.

To recap, follow this exercise:

1) Complete all your steps.
2) Open a cash ISA for money left over after paying all your outgoings.
3) Contact me to discuss taking the five-day challenge and one-to-one review about your finances.

After reading this book in its entirety, please provide a review of the book on Amazon, or with the retailer from whom you bought it.

Other Publications

Mastering Your Finance* Vol.2 - *How to Make Money Online.

This book will cover how to make money online from legal and ethical companies. Online is a jungle where there are some legal and ethical companies, but also others, who will promise to help you to make money, until they come up with excuses and stop paying you. I have created a platform, which provides the names of companies tested by me, and these companies have paid me month after month without charging me any money up front.

Mastering Your Finance* Vol.3 - *Write, Publish and Sell Your Book.

This book will cover how to write, publish and sell your books. I share my knowledge and experience and show you how to avoid my mistakes, so that you are in total control of your book and sales. I share my publisher and regain 100% royalties of your book.

Mastering Your Finance* Vol.4 - *How to Generate a Passive Income.

This book will cover how to invest in a British company which is involved in modernising properties, returning your investment plus 11% interest every year. When you have reached enough capital, I introduce a British company which teaches how to buy and rent out properties in the UK.

Other Publications

Thrumming Heart.

This is a spellbinding English collection of fantasy, sci-fi, detective, and paranormal short stories. It received a bronze medal in the Global Book Awards in 2021 and it became an Amazon best-seller in December 2022. The book is available in e-book, paperback and audio book formats. It will be available as a graphic novel in the future.

Timothy Divine and His Adventures.

This is my first English novel, and tells the story of Timothy Divine, a 10-year-old boy exploring new worlds in his rocket ship and interacting with his grandfather, Jo, and his friends. The novel has a lot of funny and emotional moments, which I am sure the reader will enjoy and share with family and friends.

Dr Victor Slater and The World.

This is my second English novel, in which the author tells how Dr Victor Slater and humanoid dinosaurs worked together in protecting Earth from the invasion of an evil alien race, Y42. In this novel, the reader will come across a love triangle, comedy and drama.

Autobiography

Paolo Debernardi was born on 3 July 1973, in Casale Monferrato (province of Alessandria) in Piedmont, but lived with his family in Mortara (province of Pavia, south-west of Milan) in Lombardy until 1997.

In June of that year, he moved to Bishopthorpe and, from there, to York, in England, where he lived until March 2001.

Because of his work he moved to Worcester, where he lived until July 2002 and, in August of the same year, he decided to transfer to Glasgow in Scotland until 2006.

He moved back to York from 2006 until 2009.

From a small child, he demonstrated his success, winning various awards in the Youth Games in Mortara, in the painting and sports competitions.

A symbolic collection of medals took him to the Collegio San Carlo di Borgo San Martino, as an accountant and commercial expert, and here he discovered his greatest loves: being a football manager helping his teams win several trophies, and poetry, through studying the French symbolists Charles Baudelaire and Arthur Rimbaud.

These two great writers aroused a passion in Paolo Debernardi and this prompted him to write innumerable poetic biographies, maxims and dedications embracing different themes and styles, to the point where they were put into a collection, together with reviews from university lecturers and writers and the drawings of Salvatore Sepe, in his first book, now out of print, entitled *Saranno state le onde del mare d'inverno...* (English translation: *It Will Be the Waves of the Sea in Winter...*) published by Edizioni Nuove Proposte U.A.O.C., (Union for Artists and Cultural workers) in Marigliano, Naples, Italy, in November 1996.

Through his poetry, Paolo Debernardi has appeared in many Italian anthologies, having taken part in several poetry competitions and won many prizes and been published in his native country.

He is also known in Germany and Australia at a local level and on the website entitled www.storymania.com.

With his move to England and the change in his mentality, Paolo Debernardi has put aside Italian literature to pursue an immense challenge, albeit a more satisfying one, of writing poetry and short stories in English, because English is a language spoken and recognized throughout the world.

Notwithstanding any difficulties, his determination and inspiration have enabled Paolo Debernardi to write English poems and short stories to such a degree of success that he came second in an English poetry competition published by the White Tower Writers Association in Doncaster, England, and first in a poetry competition published in the town of Bova Marina, Italy.

His English poems have also appeared in several anthologies in Italy, Australia, Germany, England, Switzerland and Brazil as well as on the website www.storymania.com.

In 2000, Paolo Debernardi started to write English short stories and one entitled *They Always Come Back* was published by the White Tower Writers Association in the review entitled *The Partial Eclipse*.

The three short stories entitled *They Always Come Back*, *Waiting* and *Delta Centauri* are also included on the website www.storymania.com

Besides writing this volume, Paolo Debernardi will, in the future, publish a volume of English poetry with reviews, drawings and colour photographs, entitled *Angelic Dreams*, and a volume of Italian poetry and proverbs with English translations entitled *Idyllic Paths - Sentieri Idillici*. He also plans his first English novel, *Timothy Divine and His*

Adventures, and a second English novel, *Dr Victor Slater and the World*, to be published by Debernardi Publishing.

In 2009, Paolo Debernardi published his first English short-story book entitled *The Twelve Wonders*, which is available in paperback. This book was published by AuthorHouse and it is sold in 26 countries. However this publisher stopped all the royalties. **Do not buy this book**.

In 2011, Paolo Debernardi appeared on *So You Think You Can Dance*, broadcast on BBC1, performing in front of the judges Nigel Lythgoe, Arlene Phillips, Louise Redknapp and Sisco Gomez, and meeting Cat Deeley.

In 2012, Paolo Debernardi appeared in *Got to Dance*, broadcast by Sky One, performing in front of the judges Ashley Banjo, Adam Garcia and Kimberley Wyatt.

In 2013, Paolo Debernardi appeared in *The Harry Hill Movie* as an extra.

In 2014, Paolo Debernardi appeared as an extra in *Vivid Colour* and *Prime Contact*, where his name appeared in the credits.

In 2015, Paolo Debernardi appeared as an extra in Please next, where he had a non-speaking part and his name appeared in the credits, and as an extra in Scott & Sydd.

In 2016, Paolo Debernardi appeared as an extra in Carthasys, where his name is in the credits, and in *Britain's Got Talent*. However, his audition was not broadcast by ITV1. He met Ant and Dec, Simon Cowell, Amanda Holden, Alesha Dixon, David Walliams and Stephen Mulhern.

In 2018, Paolo Debernardi was an extra in *Kings and Queens*.

In 2019, Paolo Debernardi was in the community ensemble as Mr Lipari in the play *A View From the Bridge*, by Arthur Miller, in the

York *Theatre Royal* from 20 September until 12 October and, on 15 October, he performed in a dance group. In the same year, Paolo Debernardi appeared in a short film, *Break Time*, as the main actor, Mr Davis.

In 2021, Paolo Debernardi republished his first English short story book, entitled *Thrumming Heart* in paperback, e-book and audiobook. This book won a bronze medal in the Global Book Awards, short story genre.

In 2022, *Thrumming Heart* became a best seller on Amazon.

Paolo Debernardi has met many famous people, including Ronnie O'Sullivan, Jimmy White, John Virgo, Suggs, Andy Parsons, Nikki Sanderson, Harry Hill, Sarah Jayne Dunn, Rupert Hill, Olly Murs, Richard Jones, winner of BGT 2016 and many more.

Please go to the following link for competitions, book releases, and latest updates of Paolo Debernardi's TV, film, and theatre appearances:

https://form.aweber.com/form/11/351188711.htm

www.ingramcontent.com/pod-product-compliance
Lightning Source LLC
Chambersburg PA
CBHW071525210326
41597CB00018B/2896

* 9 7 8 1 9 1 5 7 8 7 9 8 9 *